VERMONIA

The Rukan Prophecy

WALKER
BOOKS

First published in 2010 by Walker Books Ltd
87 Vauxhall Walk, London SE11 5HJ

2 4 6 8 10 9 7 5 3 1

Copyright © 2010 Raitetsu Media LLC and Ray Productions Ltd
New York and Tokyo

The right of Raitetsu Media LLC and Ray Productions Ltd to be jointly identified as authors of this work has been asserted by them in accordance with the Copyright, Designs and Patents Act 1988

This book has been typeset in CCLadronn Italic

Printed and bound in China

British Library Cataloguing in Publication Data: a catalogue record for this book is available from the British Library

ISBN 978-1-4063-2263-7

WWW.WALKER.CO.UK
WWW.VERMONIA.COM

TEMPORARILY RELEASED FROM GENERAL URO'S PRISON, MEL IS FORCED TO MOUNT THE WINGED TAKKADRA OF CAPTAIN ACIDULOUS FOR A JOURNEY TO AN UNKNOWN LOCATION.

COMPLETING A PATH SET BY QUEEN FRASINELLA,
NAOMI, NOW SEPARATED FROM DOUG, JIM, AND RAINBOW,
HAS SUCCEEDED IN RELEASING HER GUARDIAN, SUZAKU.
BURNING WITH SUZAKU'S FLAME, NAOMI LEADS FLY
AND THE UMLI PEOPLE INTO BATTLE.

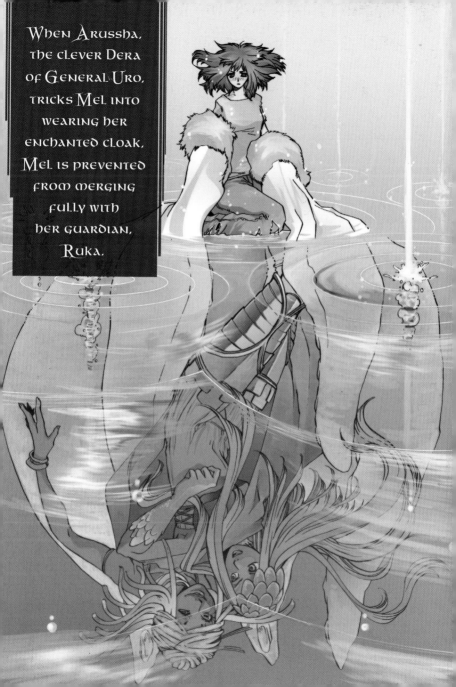

WHEN ARUSSHA,
THE CLEVER DERA
OF GENERAL URO,
TRICKS MEL INTO
WEARING HER
ENCHANTED CLOAK,
MEL IS PREVENTED
FROM MERGING
FULLY WITH
HER GUARDIAN,
RUKA.

USING THEIR
NEWFOUND POWERS
OF FIRE AND WATER,
NAOMI AND MEL
WARILY CONFRONT
EACH OTHER ON THE
BATTLEFIELD OF
THE DESTROYED
UMLI VILLAGE.

YOUR EYES WILL ADJUST.

IT'S SO BRIGHT!

BUT HURRY, THE WARRIORS ARE MAKING THE PORTAL.

NAOMI, THIS WAY.

OK, KHANN.

BUT THE ENTIRE UMLI VILLAGE HAS BEEN DESTROYED!

THERE'S HARDLY ANYTHING LEFT OF OUR HOMES NOW.

I'M GLAD SO MANY VILLAGERS SURVIVED.

I'M SO SAD TO LEAVE THIS PLACE.

WE HAVE TO TAKE AS MUCH AS WE CAN WITH US.

EVERYTHING TO REBUILD OUR LIVES.

BUT WE'LL RETURN ONE DAY. I KNOW IT.

SATORIN! KHANN! LOOK!

4

THEY'VE ALMOST COMPLETED THE PORTAL TO TAKE US TO THE TELAAM! INCREDIBLE!

YES! IT'S AMAZING! IT'S BIG ENOUGH FOR ALL THE UMLI TO PASS THROUGH SAFELY.

AWESOME!

EVERYONE, PLEASE KEEP MOVING. WE MUST HURRY.

WE CAN'T GO WITHOUT JIM AND DOUG. WHERE ARE THEY?

DO WE HAVE TO TAKE EVERYTHING FROM THE VILLAGE?

HEY! ARE YOU GUYS OK?

OH, THERE THEY ARE.

THESE WEAPONS WEIGH A TON!

YOU MUST BE NAOMI.

WHO'S
THIS?

MIKO, I THINK
IT'S TIME.

ALL RIGHT,
VULKA.

?

HERE,
TAKE THIS.

UGGH.

YES. I HAD VULKA REPAIR THE BLADE AFTER YOU BROKE IT FIGHTING THE SPIDER.

IS THIS MY SWORD?

AND IT WASN'T EASY TO DO.

MIKO GAVE ME ONLY ONE DAY TO FINISH.

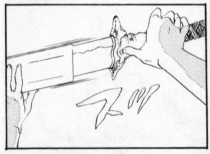

THE COLOR IS DIFFERENT. I DIDN'T HAVE ENOUGH OF THE SAME STEEL TO MAKE IT PERFECT.

SEE YOU LATER.

THANK YOU VERY MUCH.

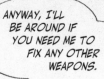

ANYWAY, I'LL BE AROUND IF YOU NEED ME TO FIX ANY OTHER WEAPONS.

VULKA IS THE LAST REMAINING BLACKSMITH OF THE UMLI.

THE LAST?

ALL THE OTHER UMLI BLACKSMITHS WERE CAPTURED BY URO'S SOLDIERS.

ALL OF THEM? NO WAY.

YES, AND WE'LL HAVE TO RESCUE THE OTHERS IF WE'RE TO MAKE THE WEAPONS WE NEED TO DEFEAT URO.

DON'T WORRY, WE WILL.

WELL, WELL, WELL.

WHAT'S THE MATTER?

VULKA, WHAT'S UP?

I NEVER WOULD HAVE THOUGHT...

THE VLESTE! THE AQAMI WARSHIP! BUTABO, COME QUICKLY!

WHAT IS IT?

ARE YOU CLOSE TO FINISHING THE REPAIRS?

WE'RE CLOSE.

SHE LOOKS ALMOST BATTLE-WORTHY.

?

YES, AND YOU'LL SOON UNDERSTAND.

...A MERMAID!

?

IRENU, DID YOU SEE THAT?

BUT WHERE'S NAOMI?

SHE'LL BE HERE SOON.

IRENU, BRING THE WARRIORS.

YES, ELDER.

IRENU!

WE MUST HURRY. THERE ISN'T MUCH TIME.

?

?

WHAT'S THE MATTER?

SELKA.

NAOMI. RAINBOW. WE'VE BEEN WAITING FOR YOU. THERE'S NO TIME TO WASTE.

???

I'M HERE, IRENU, ARE YOU READY?

I'VE BEEN SENT TO HELP YOU.

?

WE'RE READY.

I AM SELKA, GUARDIAN OF THE AQAMI. YOU MUST FOLLOW ME.

DON'T BE AFRAID.

CAN YOU MAKE THE AIR BUBBLES?

YES.

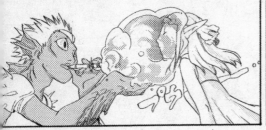

NOW YOU WILL BE ABLE TO BREATHE UNDER WATER.

LET ME MAKE ONE FOR EACH OF YOU.

EVERYONE HAS GATHERED.

I CAN SEE NAAMAN, MY GRANDFATHER, BY VODNYX'S SIDE. RUCHELLE, VODNYX'S GRANDDAUGHTER, IS THERE TOO.

NAAMAN, I HAVE BROUGHT THE WARRIORS.

HAVE THEM ENTER, IRENU.

AMAZING...

...IT'S LIKE BEING INSIDE AN AQUARIUM.

MY PEOPLE, THE POTONAWI, SING THE SAME MELODY.

RAINBOW.

WHAT A BEAUTIFUL VOICE.

THE HARMONY OF TURTLE REALM.

.....

HOW BORING IT IS TO SIT AROUND HERE WITH NOTHING TO DO.

AGH, I'VE BROKEN A NAIL.

BY THE WAY, MELANIE.

. . . . .

YOU NEVER DID TELL US WHAT YOU SAW IN YOUR LAST DREAM AFTER THE BATTLE WITH THE UMLI.

YEAH, THAT'S RIGHT! I'VE BEEN WONDERING TOO.

SAY SOMETHING!

YOU PROMISED TO TELL.

.....

MY DREAM?

IN MY DREAM I SAW MYSELF...

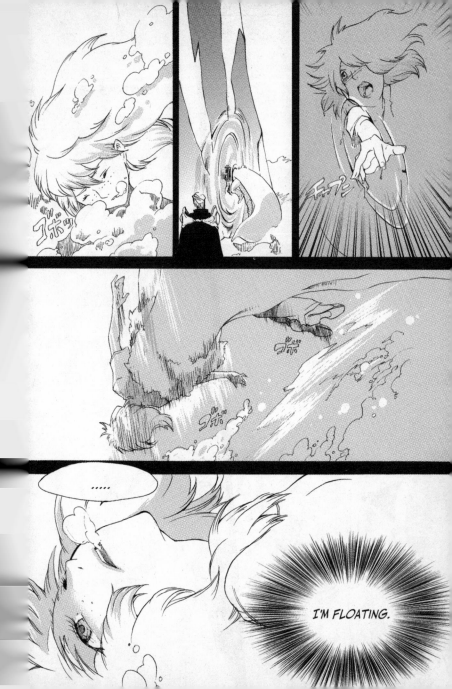

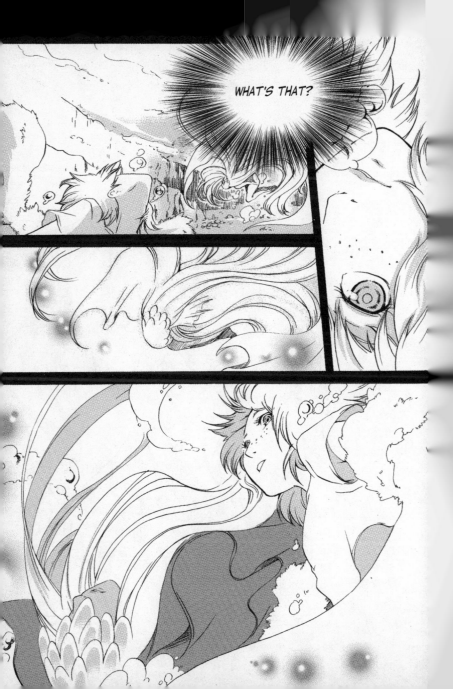

NOW LET'S FINISH GETTING RUKA'S POWER AND GET BACK.

I...

WILL I BE ABLE TO CHANGE THE FUTURE THAT RUKA HAS LET ME SEE?

I MUST FIND A WAY TO CONVINCE THE CAPTAIN TO ESCAPE WITH ME.

WE ASK THAT YOU ATTEND THE MEETING OF THE ELDERS. TRADITION DICTATES THAT YOU WEAR CEREMONIAL ATTIRE.

WARRIORS OF BLUE STAR.

DOUG, THE POTONAWI SILVER ROBES OF THUNDER.

NAOMI, THE UMLI DRESS OF FLAME.

JIM IS TO WEAR THE TELAAM CLOTHING OF THE WIND.

SOMETHING I'M TRYING TO UNDERSTAND.

BUT THERE'S SOMETHING NEW ABOUT HER.

YOU REALLY LOVE THAT SHIP, DON'T YOU?

YES, EVERYTHING ABOUT HER! HER HISTORY, HER MAGIC.

WHO'S UP THERE?

??

THE UMLI BLACKSMITH!

VULKA IS HELPING WITH THE FINAL REPAIRS.

I'D LIKE TO BE WITH HER, BUT NAAMAN REQUIRES ME TO GO ON ANOTHER MISSION.

LET US GO BACK TO THE VILLAGE. YOU MUST CHANGE.

60

HEY, WHAT'S UP WITH YOU?

NAOMI?

IT WAS AWFUL SEEING HIM DIE.

I HATED WATCHING HIS FAMILY SUFFER.

I'M THINKING ABOUT VODNYX.

WHY DOES URO WANT THIS WAR?

......

THIS IS SO BEAUTIFUL.

HOW ABOUT THIS?

WAY TOO BIG.

ALL OUR CLOTHES SEEM TO BE TOO BIG FOR YOU WARRIORS.

I'LL ADJUST IT.

THIS NECKLACE WILL WORK PERFECTLY.

DON'T MOVE, JIM.

WONDERFUL!

YOU LOOK REALLY NICE.

SATORIN!

HI, NAOMI. YOU LOOK BEAUTIFUL.

THANK YOU.

AND LITTLE CAUDACIS.

NAOMI, YOU SAVED ME FROM THE SPIDER, BUT YOU DON'T EVEN KNOW MY REAL NAME.

NAOMI, I WAS SPEAKING WITH SOLEITE, AND...

I DON'T KNOW WHY.

I'M SOLEITE. THE ELDERS WANTED ME TO BE HERE.

EACH OF THE TRIBES HAS ACCESS ONLY TO CERTAIN POWERS.

...HE TOLD ME HE HAS NEVER SEEN ANYONE LIKE ME IN THE TRIBES OF THE TURTLE REALM.

!
WHAT DO YOU MEAN?

I, FOR EXAMPLE, AM OF THE TIENTIYU AND BREATHE FIRE.

BUT SATORIN CAN WORK WITH MANY POWERS. SHOW THEM.

OK.

PLEASE, TAKE YOUR SEATS.

I'M GLAD THEY PUT US TOGETHER.

ME TOO.
I FEEL A LOT BETTER WHEN YOU'RE WITH ME.

I, NAAMAN OF THE TELAAM, AND ON BEHALF OF THE OTHER ELDERS,

WELCOME YOU ALL.

WATER, ONE OF THE PILLARS, HAS ALREADY FALLEN. VODNYX, OUR ELDER, HAS BEEN KILLED.

THIS GREAT HALL HAS NEVER SEEN A GATHERING OF SUCH IMPORTANCE. OUR BELOVED TURTLE REALM IS UNDER ATTACK.

WE CANNOT KEEP CREATING BARRIERS AND HOPING TO KEEP URO'S SOLDIERS BACK. WE'RE ALWAYS JUST DEFENDING OURSELVES.

WE HAVE COME HERE TO FIGHT WITH YOU AND FIND OUR FRIEND. WE HAVE TO FIGHT TO PROTECT THOSE WHO MATTER MOST TO US, AND TO PROTECT WHAT'S MOST IMPORTANT IN THIS REALM.

WE'VE FOUGHT HIS SOLDIERS TWICE!

I AGREE!

!!!

NOW WE HAVE TO GO ON THE ATTACK...

AND EACH TIME WE GAINED STRENGTH AND MADE THEM RETREAT.

...TO WIN.

77

WE FIGHT WELL BECAUSE WE DO NOT FIGHT ALONE.

EACH ONE OF US HAS BEEN TOUCHED BY A GUARDIAN!

I, BY THE SILVER TIGER, RAITETSU. JIM, BY THE WINGED PANTHER, SUIRAN. AND NAOMI, BY THE RED PHOENIX, SUZAKU.

BUT IF RAITETSU,

SUIRAN,

SUZAKU,

AND RUKA...

MEL HAS HER GUARDIAN TOO. BUT WE BELIEVE URO CONTROLS RUKA.

YES, IN THIS WAY WE COULD PROTECT THE SACRED BOLIRIUM. THE BOLIRIUM WOULD BE ABLE TO RESTORE THE LOST PILLAR.

...COULD ALL FOUR FIGHT TOGETHER, WE COULD STOP URO.

78

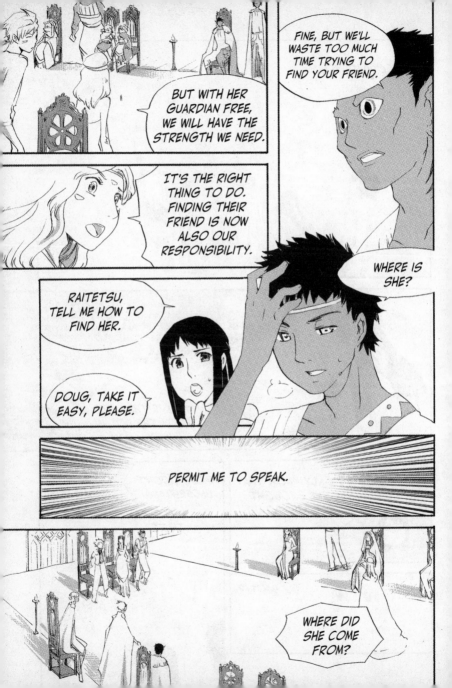

BEFORE THE DESTRUCTION OF OUR PLANET, MY QUEEN BID ME WATCH OVER YOU.

QUEEN FRASINELLA?

WHAT I DO KNOW, IS THAT YOU, ALONG WITH THE FOUR VERAS AND THE FOUR MINISTERS, WERE CHOSEN TO LEAVE VERMONIA.

WHY? WHAT AM I SUPPOSED TO DO?

EVEN I DO NOT KNOW.

SATORIN...

I HEARD THAT VOICE IN BATTLE.

SEVERAL TIMES...

SHE HELPED ME IN THE FIGHT.

...I FELT COMPELLED TO COME TO YOUR AID.

THIS ISN'T SUZAKU!

URO'S TROOPS ARE LAUNCHING A NEW ATTACK AGAINST TWO MORE PILLARS.

NOW THEY ARE ALSO TARGETING SATORIN.

84

YOU MEAN THAT THE LITTLE CREATURE WAS INSIDE THE EGG ZANNI BROUGHT FROM VERMONIA?

SO IT WOULD SEEM, MY CAPTAIN.

I WILL CONTINUE TO FIND WAYS TO LEARN ABOUT THEIR DEFENSES AND BRING YOU INFORMATION.

DESTROY THE PILLARS AND BRING ME THE ONE CALLED SATORIN.

CAPTAIN!

!!!

YES, MY GENERAL.

SIR.

I'M AFRAID URO WILL LOSE PATIENCE...

WE CAN'T AFFORD TO FAIL AGAIN.

???

WHAT'S THE CAPTAIN DOING?

ズウ

WHO'S THERE?

WATCH OUT!

PLOP

HEY!

HI.

YOU'VE CHANGED
YOUR CLOTHES.

YEAH,
IRENU GAVE
ME THESE.

SATORIN...

BUT I CAN'T UNDERSTAND HOW ZANNI KNOWS THE THINGS SHE DOES.

YOU'RE RIGHT, BUT THAT'S WHY YOU HAVE TO BE ESPECIALLY CAREFUL.

I WILL.

I'M CONFUSED. I'M NOT FROM BLUE STAR, NOR OF THE TURTLE REALM.

.....

I'M NOT SURE WHO YOU BELONG TO, SATORIN. AND I DON'T CARE.

YOU'RE MY FRIEND!

THAT'S ALL THAT MATTERS TO ME.

COME ON, EVERYONE.

ARE YOU ALL READY?

112

IF YOU'RE ATTACKED, SEND YOUR THOUGHTS TO US. LUCKILY WE HAVE RAITETSU'S ROKOLOI TO COMMUNICATE WITH FLY AND NAOMI TOO.

IT HAS TO HOLD AT LEAST UNTIL YOU SECURE THE CORE.

AGREED.

THE REST OF YOU, COME WITH ME.

HURRY.

WE MUSTN'T LET THE ISLAND FALL INTO URO'S HANDS.

REALLY?

YOU KNOW, THE VLESTE IS PARTLY MADE FROM XANDAN WOOD.

I'VE NEVER BEEN HERE BEFORE, BUT THE BARDS HAVE SUNG OF THE CORE.

WE'LL BUILD ANOTHER SHIELD TO PROTECT THE FORCE OF THUNDER.

BUTABO, SHOULD WE TAKE THIS PATH DOWN?

YES, I THINK SO.

IT'S WAY TOO HOT HERE.

.....

ARE YOU ALL RIGHT, RAINBOW?

YEAH, I'M OK.

I HAVE WATER FOR WHOEVER NEEDS SOME.

GOOD.

WE'RE GETTING CLOSE. WE SHOULD BE THERE SOON.

I HOPE URO'S SOLDIERS HAVEN'T GOTTEN THERE BEFORE US.

THE SIGNAL OF DANGER!

SUZAKU'S FEATHER!

!!

WATCH OUT!
SOMETHING'S COMING
TOWARD US!

YOU CAN'T HURT ME WITH SUCH A LITTLE KNIFE...

!!!

YOU'RE A MEMBER OF THAT TRIBE, AREN'T YOU?

THAT WAS THE DAY WE CAPTURED THE BOY FOR URO.

WE HAD A LOT OF FUN.

YOU WERE THERE WHEN MY BROTHER, FOREST, WENT MISSING?

ON THAT DAY?

IT CAN'T BE.

WHEN WE WERE ESCAPING.

NOW...

NOOOO!!

YOU... KILLED HER?

I CAN'T BELIEVE THAT'S THE SAME DAY THAT FOREST WAS TAKEN.

I BECAME HER, AND NOW, LOOK LIKE HER!

YOU HAVE TO COME WITH ME TO A SAFE PLACE.

WE HAVE TO LEAVE. YOU'RE IN DANGER.

!!

RAINBOW! FOREST!

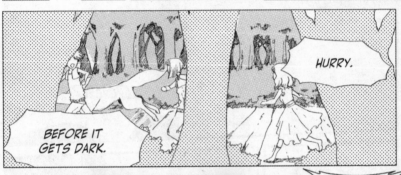

BEFORE IT GETS DARK.

HURRY.

I CAN'T GO FASTER!

WAIT FOR ME, FLY!

WHERE ARE YOU?

WHO'S THERE?

NOOOO!!

WHAT...?!

138

NAOMI!

...THEN YOU'LL BECOME URO'S ENEMY, AND HE'LL DESTROY YOU.

BUT IF YOU LOOK LIKE ME...

DESTROY ME? WHY?

STOP!!

BECAUSE URO WILL THINK YOU'RE ONE OF US! AND WE PROTECT THE PILLARS.

THAT DOESN'T MATTER TO ME.

I ONLY CARE ABOUT HOW YOU CAN HELP ME LOOK LIKE YOU. YOUR PRETTINESS WILL JOIN WITH MINE.

AGHH!!

THAT'S ENOUGH.

SUZAKU!!!!

THE MONSTER DISAPPEARED...

EVERYTHING IS SHAKING!

...INTO THE GROUND!

I'LL GET YOU.

RIGHT BELOW US!

EVERYONE, COVER YOUR EARS!

YOU'RE RIGHT.

SINGERS, READY?

YES!

MY EARS!

CAN YOU STILL FIGHT?

OF COURSE.

IS HE OK?

KHANN!

OK.

WE HAVE TO COME UP WITH A PLAN.

TELL US WHEN YOU'VE FOUND HER!

NAOMI, YOU'LL HAVE TO LOOK DOWN AND TELL US EXACTLY WHERE SHE'S GOING TO BREAK THROUGH.

OK, AND YOU MUST FORM THE NET TO TRAP HER.

154

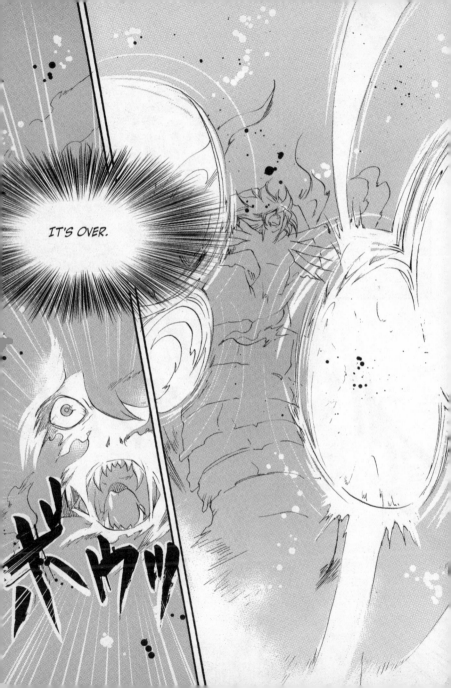

BRING IT ON,
URO.
NOTHING
YOU HAVE
CAN DEFEAT US.

THEY'RE ATTACKING!

URO'S ARMY IS ALREADY THERE!

MEL?

THERE'S NOTHING YOU CAN DO HERE,

IT'S OVER.

THIS IS YOUR WORK!

I COULDN'T HAVE DONE THIS ON MY OWN.

LOOK OVER THERE.

THIS NEEDED
THE DERAS.

THIS WAS YAMI MAGIC.
THE SOLDIERS
DESTROYED
EVERYTHING.

DO YOU THINK
I COULD HAVE
STOPPED THEM?

EVERYTHING?

YES, THAT'S
WHAT THEY
DO.

COME ON!
HURRY!

WATCH YOUR STEP.

IT LOOKS SO DEEP!

JIM...

YES, ALTHOUGH WE DON'T KNOW HOW.

IS THAT THE CORE THAT MAKES THE ISLAND FLOAT?

?

ME? NO.

DID YOU JUST CALL ME?

HMM.

I COULD HAVE SWORN I HEARD SOMEONE CALLING.

HELP ME...

HELP ME, JIM!!

JIM?

OK, I DID NOT IMAGINE IT!

.....

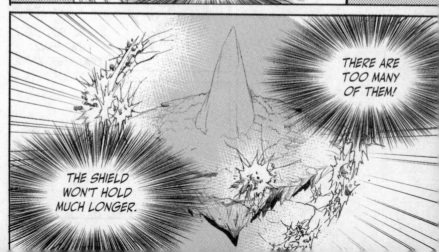

...IF THIS ROCK IS PART OF THE CORE...

HOW COME?

WELL, MAYBE...

...AND THE CORE IS THUNDER, MAYBE RAITETSU...

JIM!!

WHATEVER. THERE'S NO TIME.

WHAT?

I EITHER HOLD UP THE ROCK...

...OR I DROP IT ON JIM.

RAINBOW'S DOWN THERE.

...I HAVE TO TAKE IT WITH ME.

I GUESS I HAVE NO CHOICE...

I CAN SEE THE LAKE.

I HOPE I'M IN TIME.

THE BOULDERS ARE GOING TO FALL INTO THE LAKE!

HOLD ON TO IT A LITTLE LONGER.

NO!! RAINBOW'S HERE. I CAN'T GET HER OUT!!

??!

JIM! REMEMBER WHAT BUTABO SAID!

THE BARRIER'S GETTING STRONGER.

IRENU, THE FLAME OF THE DESERT.

OH, NO!

WE'VE LOST A SECOND PILLAR.

WE WEREN'T ABLE TO PROTECT IT.

IRENU!!

ALLOWING ME IN, PUTS YOU ALL IN DANGER!

WHY DID YOU BRING ME HERE?

DON'T MOVE.

WHAT DO YOU MEAN?

DON'T WORRY, YOU'RE SAFE, THAT'S WHAT COUNTS.

NAOMI!

WE'LL TAKE CARE OF WHATEVER COMES.

!!!!

THEY'RE HERE!

SATORIN, GET HIM OUT OF THE LAKE IMMEDIATELY!

DOUG CAN'T HOLD ON ANY LONGER, YOU NEED TO GET OUT OF THERE!

HUFF

HUFF

JIM!!

NO!!!!